Kids
London

**black dog
publishing**
london uk

D0715345

Contents

5 Introduction

6 In The Area

8 Notting Hill
12 Kensington and Chelsea
16 Shoreditch
20 The South Bank
24 Dulwich

30 Outdoors & Nature

32 Animals

33 Spitalfields Farm
34 SEA LIFE London Aquarium
38 Battersea Park Children's Zoo
40 London Zoo
42 Vauxhall City Farm

46 Outdoors

47 Clissold Park
48 Kew Gardens
50 Crystal Palace Park
54 London Wetland Centre
56 New River Walk Path
58 Nature Play
60 Victoria Park
64 Gunnersbury Nature Triangle

66 Arts & Entertainment

68 Film

69 BFI FUNdays
70 Rich Mix
72 Ritzy

74 Storytelling

75 Tales on Moon Lane
76 Barbican Children's Library
78 The National Gallery
80 Discover Children's Story Centre

84 Theatres

85 artsdepot
86 Battersea Arts Centre
90 Little Angel Theatre
91 Puppet Theatre Barge
92 Polka Theatre

96 Creating Things

97 Little Hands Design
98 ZEBRA Ceramics
100 The Strings Club
102 The Kids' Cookery School
103 ARTBASH
106 The Creation Station
108 The Big Draw

110 Activities & Leisure

112 Playgrounds

113   Shakespeare Walk Adventure
       Playground
114   The Diana Memorial Playground
118   Coram's Fields
119   The Bees Knees
120   The Wild Kingdom

122 Swimming

123   London Fields Lido
124   Hampstead Heath
126   Diana, Princess of Wales
       Memorial Fountain
128   Oasis Sports Centre
129   Leyton Leisure Lagoon
130   London Aquatics Centre

132 Sport

133   Hyde Park Stables
134   Brooklyn Bowl
135   Roller Disco
136   National Centre for Circus Arts
138   Laburnum Boat Club
142   The Castle Climbing Centre
144   Alexandra Palace

146 Sightseeing

148 Tours

149   London RIB Voyages
150   Treasure Trails
152   TFL Buses
153   London Duck Tours
156   Muggle Tour
158   Original Tours

160 Museums

161   Museum of London Docklands
162   London Transport Museum
164   The Hunterian Museum
166   Natural History Museum
168   The Ragged School Museum
172   Tower of London
174   The Charles Dickens Museum
176   Horniman Museum and Gardens

180 Maps

190 Image Credits

191 Acknowledgements

Introduction

London can be a boundless adventure for children and those accompanying them. With ever evolving, innovative activities and a limitless list of family-friendly classics, there is something for kids in every corner of the capital.

From prominent museums, exciting leisure activities and the open spaces of the city's largest parks, to hands-on creative clubs, annual festivals and little things to keep an eye out for, *Kids London* is an anthology of ideas and inspiration for places to visit and things to do with children up to the age of 14.

Many of the entries listed here are unique, while others are representative of an activity available at various outlets across the capital (in instances of which we have picked our favourite examples, or those that offer something special, different or extra). Most of the institutions profiled have a schedule of changing exhibitions and interactive activities, ranging from storytelling to handling exhibits, so make sure to check out the listed websites for the latest programmes. It is also worth noting that some of the activities featured here are transient or move around the city, and that opening times vary between each organisation featured, so be sure to check the websites for further relevant information.

A number of features, including full contact details in each profile and an illustrated map section with location points for every activity or organisation, should help you plan your fun in the city. In addition, several "In The Area" guides outline five locations—Notting Hill, Kensington and Chelsea, Shoreditch, the South Bank, and Dulwich—that are filled with nearby activities and attractions. For the contact details of activities and organisations mentioned in this section, see the miniature directory following it, and for the map locations, look for points outlined in red.

In The Area

NORTH

WEST

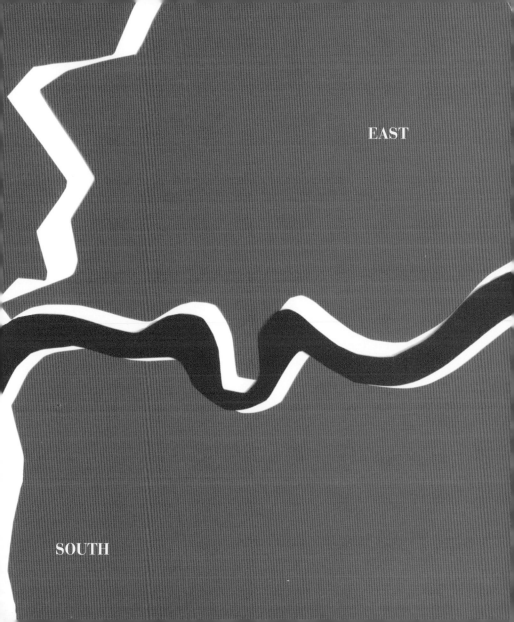

Notting Hill

Well-loved for its bohemian personality, lively multicultural community and wide scope of artistic talent, Notting Hill is a vibrant urban village in which to spend some time with the kids.

A long list of child-friendly eating options include: the Electric Diner at the Electric Cinema (grab breakfast on Saturday mornings before catching a kids' film—a pretty luxurious experience if you pre-book a double bed from which to watch the movie!); the full American diner experience—complete with classic American menu staples, milkshakes and of course rock-and-roll music—found at Sticky Fingers, a restaurant founded by Rolling Stone Bill Wyman; and of course, the colourful food stalls and pop-up eateries of Portobello Road market.

Alongside the animated and fragrant food stall options, this notorious London landmark is home to over 1,000 other stands, selling a huge range of items from quirky fashion items to music, though specialising no doubt in antiques. Why not try bartering with the best of them at some of the many toy or children's clothing vendors? Alternatively, stop by some of the area's surrounding permanent shops; Honeyjam is an adorable little institution specialising in traditional and retro toys— think wooden building blocks, traditional teddies and fancy dress outfits.

Besides the toy stalls and inevitable sweet treats, appeal lies in the exuberant atmosphere of the market, which is often dotted with live music and street performers. Be aware though, Portobello Road can get extremely busy, so arrive early to avoid the crowds. The market opening and closing times vary from stall to stall so check the website before you set off.

The August Bank Holiday brings with it the Notting Hill Carnival (one of the largest street festivals in Europe), an all-singing, all-dancing and all-glittering celebration of Caribbean culture and history. Family Day—typically

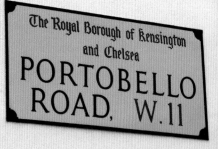

The Royal Borough of Kensington and Chelsea

PORTOBELLO ROAD, W.11

Sunday—is the best day to take along the children to watch the flamboyant parade, dance to great live music and eat an assortment of exotic food.

Notting Hill's somewhat more grown-up and affluent neighbour is leafy and relaxing Holland Park—a wonderful place to stroll through with the family, and a good place to escape to after Notting Hill's noisy bustle. The park proper contains an adventure playground (with a large zip-wire) and stunning grounds, as well as Japanese-style Kyoto gardens, complete with a waterfall, koi carp and a number of roaming peacocks (if you are lucky you might even find a stray feather or two). In the summer the park also hosts a number of outdoor theatre productions, which are well worth keeping an eye out for.

Kensington and Chelsea

With plenty of museums, parks and restaurants within walking distance or just a quick bus ride away, the "Royal Borough" of Kensington and Chelsea is a particularly family-friendly slice of London.

The Kings Road is a good place to start. This smart high street is home to top-notch, high-end children's toy and clothes stores, as well as plenty of child-friendly cafes and restaurants, including My Old Dutch, a quirky place entirely devoted to pancakes both sweet and savoury—essential eating for any little pancake enthusiast.

The Saatchi Gallery is just one of Kensington and Chelsea's catalogue of museums and galleries in which to keep the family entertained. Situated just off the Kings Road's main stretch, this contemporary collection is free to enter (though one-off exhibitions may have an entrance fee). On Exhibition Road—just a ten minute bus ride away—is a bumper selection of London's major museums. Sat amongst the Natural History Museum (p 166) and the Victoria and Albert Museum, the Science Museum is an excellent place to spend a day with the kids. As well as an extensive and enlightening range of enjoyable and educational galleries, such as the Pattern Pod—a multi-sensory gallery allowing children to explore different patterns around the world—the Science Museum houses its very own Imax cinema, showcasing science-themed 3D films. Much of the Museum is free to enter, but fees apply to some exhibitions and the Imax.

If you would prefer not be stuck indoors, the area also boasts plenty of pleasant outdoor spaces. The Chelsea Physic Gardens—just a 15 minute walk from Sloane Square station, or a quick bus ride straight there—is home to a walled garden that overflows with flowers and greenery. Founded in 1673, Chelsea Physic Gardens have a rich history as one of London's most famous natural medicine gardens. In fact amongst the Gardens' collection of over 5,000 plant species there are still numerous medicinal plants and herbs. There are a number of family activities on offer that will engage and educate your children about nature and the use of plants, and, after a run around the Gardens, there is coffee and cake waiting at the Tangerine Dream Cafe. Tickets to the Gardens are £9.90 for adults and £6.60 for children (those under five go free). It is worth noting that the Gardens are closed on Saturdays.

Nearby Knightsbridge—famous for luxury department store Harrods, where you can do some heavy duty window shopping in the toy department—is just five minutes from Hyde Park. As well as summertime fun boating on the Serpentine, cooling off in the paddling pool or letting loose in the children's playground, you can visit Hyde Park's winter fair from November to January. At Winter Wonderland there are rides, German market food stalls and general Christmas-themed fun, such as ice-skating, a Magical Ice Kingdom, Santa Land and Circus shows. Entry is free except for certain attractions, where pre-booking is advised.

Shoreditch

Based around an approximately 1.2 mile-long stretch of the Regent's Canal, packed with parks and playgrounds, an outdoor swimming pool, city farm, street market and the canal, this part of Shoreditch is the perfect plot for getting kids outdoors.

On Kingsland Road, just near Hoxton Rail Station, is the Geffrye Museum, a collection of different domestic interiors typical of various eras throughout London's history. Take a tour around the 11 period living spaces and have a look at the décor, furniture and toys of the past! Make sure to visit the period gardens at the Museum too.

Hoxton Street Monster Supplies store, a unique shop selling all manner of off-putting produce for any little monster, from tins of a "vague sense of unease" to cubed earwax, is on nearby Hoxton Street. This quirky cabinet of curiosities is ran in collaboration with (and raises funds for) the Ministry of Stories, a creative writing and mentoring charity for young people in East London. A visit here, and perhaps a ghastly treat to take away, will get the creative juices flowing in your kids, while aiding the imagination of young people in one of the city's poorest areas.

A short walk from Hoxton Street is Shoreditch Park— a large open space, carved out during the Blitz. Now a host of sporting facilities, including pitches for football and rugby, tennis courts and two giant boulders for harness-free rock climbing, and an adventure playground in its southwest corner make the park a great place to spend some time outdoors.

Walking along the canal path (which can be accessed just north of Shoreditch Park), you can take in more fresh air and a little nature too; alongside the canal boats, you are likely here to catch glimpses of the canal's resident wildlife: fish, swans, coots and ducks, among others. You can see more animals at Hackney City Farm, including pigs, donkeys and goats, as well as smaller, more petting-friendly creatures, such as guinea pigs and rabbits. The Farm hosts all manner of fun activities for children, and at the weekend it welcomes young volunteers (aged eight and up), enrolling them in the workings of the Farm and the care of the animals.

Hackney City Farm is also home to a lovely family-friendly cafe, and, walking further east along the canal, you will reach another lunch- or tea-time option for a day in the area. The floating seating area of the increasingly popular Towpath Cafe is a great setting for lunch with the family, and their simple but tasty food will hit the spot.

More food is on offer at Broadway Market (further along the canal, exiting left). Every Saturday this pretty street fills with stalls selling everything from organic and free-range produce, to delectable home-baked cakes and tarts, to a mouth-watering selection of hot on-the-spot meals and snacks.

At the top of Broadway Market is yet another park. London Fields Park is fairly small but contains, on its western edge, London Fields Lido (p 123).

The South Bank

A vast selection of galleries and museums, places to eat, great views and a lively mix of people, as well as pop-up events—such as an annual Christmas market—make the Thames' South Bank the perfect place to spend a day with the kids.

The stretch between the Hungerford and the wobbly Millennium Bridges (approximately 1 mile long) is particularly packed with fun free or affordable activities. Starting from Hungerford Bridge, walking along the bank-side promenade you will see an array of lively street performers—you can even catch a performance of a different kind at the skateboarding park carved into the crevice underneath the iconic concrete structure, the Hayward Gallery. Next to the Gallery's entrance and cafe is the home to its summer resident sculpture: Appearing Rooms, by Jeppe Hien. The piece—a floor fountain, from which water jets up and falls back down in a series of constellations to form changing constructions you can dart in and out of—captivates little children who appear annually in their bathing suits ready to take on, and cool off in, the art work.

A little way along the stretch is Gabriel's Wharf. Filled with quaint, pastel-shaded shop fronts and restaurants—giving the overall impression of a seaside resort—and carved wooden animal-shaped stools, this colourful spot is an excellent place to grab an ice cream and a sit-down. Continuing along the river, past the OXO Tower, you will come to Tate Modern. This London favourite is filled with an exceptional permanent collection (as well as changing

feature shows and a couple of extensive art book and souvenir shops), and regularly hosts events for children. Very little kids may be impressed enough with the building itself; the gallery's vast Turbine Hall—its name retained since the building's previous incarnation as the Bankside Power Station—is lined with smooth, sloping concrete for lolling, bouncing and charging around on. From outside, look out for the Peregrine Falcons that live up high in the Tate's chimney!

If you aren't afraid of getting gritty, the Thames riverbank in front of Shakespeare's Globe Theatre (just minutes from the Tate Modern) is the perfect place for first-time beachcombers. You can find your own treasures from London's history alongside the serious mudlarkers who comb this area. The Thames' oxygen-free mud preserves items dropped in the river, making it the perfect place to find a historical gem. Make sure to follow the beachcombers' guides though: to dig or scrape away at the surface, you need to contact the Port of London Authority (PLA) first, and anything interesting you find should be registered with the Museum of London.

It is also important to follow several highly recommended safety procedures when beachcombing. Firstly, check the tide times; tides on the Thames can come in and out quickly. Check a tide timetable before you go, and when you find a spot to sift in, make sure you know your exit points, particularly with children who will need to be able to get up and down steps that may be slippery (information for safety, tide timetables, and maps are all available on the PLA website). Second, there's a risk when handling items, mud or water from the Thames, in which various diseases can be carried. Don't let children touch their face, eyes or mouth when beachcombing, or better still, use waterproof gloves. Hand sanitiser can help, but wash your hands as soon as possible afterwards to be safe. If you are going to be prepared, you'll need waterproof trousers and good, non-slip shoes, as well as a bag to keep all of your treasures in.

When you get peckish, there are child-friendly cafes in both Tate Modern and the Royal Festival Hall (part of the cultural hub, the Southbank Centre), as well as plenty of branches of popular casual restaurants around the Hayward Gallery, and in the summer the area fills with pop-up food stalls and ice-cream vendors.

Dulwich

Quaint and pretty Dulwich Village is a little slice of proper village life in the city. The village itself is lined with nice shops and kid-friendly restaurants. Family orientated establishments include cosy Rocca-di Papas, where you can grab some no-frills classic Italian food, and Dulwich Park's Pavilion Cafe.

While in Dulwich Park, get out on the water at one of the ponds; rowing boats and pedalos can be hired from April to October. You can also borrow an array of interesting bikes from the Park's resident bike hire joint, London Recumbents. Children will love racing through the park on extraordinary bikes from a selection that includes tandems, Banana Bikes, Robin Trikes, and of course, recumbents (an ergonomic bike on which the rider reclines low to the ground in a bucket seat, peddling with legs extended in front). Serious cyclists will love visiting the Herne Hill Velodrome. Pop-in public sessions are affordable, safe and open to all, and a variety of Kids' Clubs offer the chance to improve and compete.

If boats and bikes aren't enough, in nearby Brockwell Park, there is a miniature railway. The little trains on this track (a cute collection of steam engines and trams) take their passengers of all ages on a magical ride from the Herne Hill gates to Brockwell Lido and back again. The Brockwell Miniature Railway operates from March to October and costs only £1 per passenger (those under two ride for free).

Museums in the area include the Dulwich Picture Gallery and the Horniman Museum. The former—London's first purpose-built gallery—is rich with Old Master paintings and offers a number of family activities, such as "ArtPlay" and "Gallery Stories". The latter, the Horniman Museum, is a South London institution comprising a trove of zoological treasures, an aquarium, gardens and a programme of events (see p 176).

Lying a little south of Dulwich is one of the largest remaining fragments of the Great North Wood—a historical natural oak forest. Sydenham Hill Woods provide a welcome escape from urban life and a chance to learn all about nature. Kids will love spying wildlife and exploring the outdoors, something that the organisers of Nature Play know well (see p 58).

Crystal Palace Park is a short bus-hop a little further south from Dulwich. Here, as well as a farm and various sporting facilities, are a family of very unusual London residents: the Crystal Palace dinosaurs (see p 50).

Notting Hill

 Electric Diner
191 Portobello Road
London, W11 2ED

0207 908 9696
www.electricdiner.com

Electric Cinema
191 Portobello Road
London, W11 2ED

0207 908 9696
www.electriccinema.co.uk

Sticky Fingers
1A Phillimore Gardens
London, W8 7QB

020 7938 5338
www.stickyfingers.co.uk

Portobello Road market
Portobello Road
London, W10 5TA

0207 727 7684
www.portobelloroad.co.uk

 Honeyjam
2 Blenheim Crescent
London, W11 1NN

0207 243 0449
www.honeyjam.co.uk

Holland Park
Ilchester Place
W8

http://www.rbkc.gov.uk

Kensington and Chelsea

My Old Dutch
221 Kings Road
Chelsea
London, SW3 5EJ

0207 376 5650
www.myolddutch.com

Saatchi Gallery
Duke of York's HQ
King's Road
London, SW3 4RY

0208 968 9331
www.saatchigallery.com

Victoria and Albert Museum
Cromwell Road
London, SW7 2RL

0207 942 2000
www.vam.ac.uk

The Science Museum
Exhibition Road
South Kensington
London, SW7 2DD

020 7942 4000
www.sciencemuseum.org.uk

 Chelsea Physic Gardens
66 Royal Hospital Road
Chelsea
London, SW3 4HS

0207 352 5646
www.chelseaphysicgarden.co.uk

 Harrods
87–135, Brompton Road
Knightsbridge
London, SW1X 7XL

0207 730 1234
www.harrods.com

Hyde Park
W2 2UH

www.royalparks.org.uk

Winter Wonderland
Hyde Park
London, W2 2UH

www.hydeparkwinterwonderland.com

Shoreditch

The Geffrye Museum
136 Kingsland Road
London, E2 8EA

0207 739 9893
www.geffrye-museum.org.uk

 Hoxton Street Monster Supplies Store
159 Hoxton Street
London, N1 6PJ

0207 729 4159
www.monstersupplies.org

(17) Shoreditch Park
New North Road
N1 6TA

0208 356 3000
www.hackney.gov.uk/shoreditch
-park.htm

(18) Hackney City Farm
1a Goldsmiths Row
London, E2 8QA

0207 729 6381
www.hackneycityfarm.co.uk

(19) Towpath Cafe
Regent's Canal towpath
between Whitmore Bridge
and Kingsland Road Bridge
London, N1 5SB

(20) Broadway Market
London, E8 4PH

07709 311869
www.broadwaymarket.co.uk

The South Bank

(21) South Bank Christmas Market
Belvedere Road
London, SE1 8X

(22) Hayward Gallery
Southbank Centre
Belvedere Road
London, SE1 8XX

0207 960 4200
www.southbankcentre.co.uk/
venues/hayward-gallery

(23) Gabriel's Wharf
Upper Ground
London, SE1 9PP

(24) Tate Modern
Bankside
London, SE1 9TG

0207 887 8888
www.tate.org.uk/visit/tate-modern

(25) Shakespeare's Globe
21 New Globe Walk
Bankside
London, SE1 9DT

020 7902 1400
www.shakespearesglobe.com

Dulwich

(26) Rocca-di Papas
75–79 Dulwich Village
London, SE21 7BJ

0208 299 6333
www.roccarestaurants.com/
menus.htm

(27) Dulwich Park Pavillion Cafe
Dulwich Park, off College Road
London, SE21 7BQ

0208 299 1383
www.the-pavillion-café.com

(28) Dulwich Park
Dulwich Park, off College Road
London, SE21 7BQ

(29) London Recumbents
Rangers Yard
Dulwich Park
College Road
London, SE21 7BQ

020 7708 5464
www.londonrecumbents.co.uk/
bikes_we_hire.html

(30) Brockwell Park
Dulwich Road
London, SE24 0PA

(31) Dulwich Picture Gallery
Gallery Road
London, SE21 7AD

020 8693 5254
www.dulwichpicturegallery.org.uk

(32) Herne Hill Velodrome
104 Burbage Road
Herne Hill
London, SE24 9HE

www.hernehillvelodrome.com

Outdoors & Nature

Animals

➊ Spitalfields Farm

Spitalfields Farm is a little slice of the countryside right in the heart of the city. The Farm promotes animal welfare, a cause they are fittingly occupied with; from ducks, geese, sheep, ponies, pigs and ferrets, to favourites Bayleaf the donkey and Bentley the goat, Spitalfields is home to an entire menagerie of its own. Originally set up by volunteers in 1978, Spitalfields continues to be largely dependent on voluntary farm keepers. In addition to various meet-the-animal events, it hosts a summer market and a cafe, open every Sunday throughout the summer months.

Spitalfields Farm
Buxton Street
London, E1 5AR

020 7247 8762
www.spitalfieldscityfarm.org

❷ SEA LIFE London Aquarium

SEA LIFE London Aquarium
County Hall
Westminster Bridge Road
London, SE1 7PB

0871 663 1678
www.visitsealife.com/london/

The SEA LIFE London Aquarium might be a major feature on the London tourist hit list—with hefty entry prices, shuffling crowds and massive gift shop to match— but it's an undeniably great place to take inquisitive young minds. Based in the old County Hall building on the South Bank, the Aquarium holds one of Europe's largest collections of global marine life; over 500 specimens include sharks, stingrays, turtles, clownfish, octopus and penguins, amongst many others.

Geared up for family exploration, 14 themed zones feature playful, if somewhat plastic, creations which are meant to evoke the Aquarium's residents' native habitats. There are numerous photo opportunities along the way, interactive information points and even an area where little hands can touch starfish and other water creatures.

❸ Battersea Park Children's Zoo

Battersea Park Children's Zoo
Battersea Park
Chelsea Bridge
London, SW11 4NJ

020 7924 5826
www.batterseaparkzoo.co.uk

In central London's Battersea Park there is a miniature zoo created entirely with young visitors in mind. Battersea Park Children's Zoo is home to a whole family of animals from common farm animals such as donkeys, rabbits and chickens, to rather more exotic bearded dragon lizards, snakes, monkeys, wallabies, emu, coati, parrots and ring-tailed lemurs. Children will also have lots of fun spotting meerkats from the secret lookout tunnel or otters splashing about in the pond, and could even have a go at feeding some of the animals in the on-site Barley Mow Farm. If all of that doesn't tire them out there is an adventure playground complete with sand and water play areas, a real tractor and a life-sized fire engine.

The zoo and playground are open all year round, hosting various events throughout the year, from Hedgehog or Snake Days to "Monkey Mayhem", Halloween fun days and Easter Egg hunts.

④ London Zoo

London Zoo is one of London's classic family destinations. You may have to consider the downsides of very popular inner-city attractions—go on a bank holiday and expect a fair chunk of the experience to be queuing to get into the park—but there's no doubt that the zoo has a lot to offer. This huge zoo in Regent's Park is home to many species including monkeys, meerkats, otters, gorillas, giraffes, zebras, warthogs, crocodiles, snakes, lizards and big cats—lions, tigers and servals. Perhaps the stars of the show are the residents of Penguin Beach, England's biggest penguin pool. Visitors can watch the Zoo's Humboldt and Macaroni penguins waddle around their beach, or, through the underwater viewing areas, see them dive for their fish dinners during the twice-daily feeding sessions.

There are also plenty of options if you want to do something a little more special at the zoo: for an additional fee you can "meet" some of the animals, and 11–15 year olds can try their hands at being a Junior Keeper for a day.

London Zoo
Regent's Park
London, NW1 4RY

0207 449 6200
www.zsl.org/zsl-london-zoo

⑤ Vauxhall City Farm

Vauxhall City Farm
165 Tyers Street
London, SE11 5HS

0207 582 4204
www.vauxhallcityfarm.org

Amongst an award-winning selection of farm animals that includes pigs, goats, alpacas, ferrets, guinea pigs and rare-breed sheep, Vauxhall City Farm is also home to horses and ponies, which make up a small riding school. At the Farm, kids as young as four can learn how to ride and take care of the animals, giving them a taste of the country.

There are lots of things for children at the Farm besides viewing and petting the animals. For example, they can get their hands dirty being a farmer for a day—a programme aimed at young people between age eight and 14—feeding, grooming and mucking out the animals. At the end of the day, they will come away with a certificate and rosette for their efforts. And if that's not enough for your budding farmer, Vauxhall City Farm has its own long-running Young Farmers Club. Anybody aged between eight and 18 is welcome to join up and help with all of the important work around the farm. Young Farmers gain a number of skills while having a fun, social experience.

For other horse riding options, see p 133.

Outdoors

❶ Clissold Park

Clissold Park's locals are probably happy that nearby Finsbury Park is somewhat better known though the former, moments off Stoke Newington's picturesque Church Street, arguably has much more to offer—all set against Clissold House, the Grade II listed central feature of the park from which the cafe now operates. As well as plenty of open green space for summer-time rounds of Frisby, the park has numerous sports grounds (some multipurpose, some dedicated tennis courts), ping pong tables, a miniature skate park, children's open air paddling pool and an impressive play area. The park has also been home to various animals for over 100 years; today two large ponds are filled with ducks and more exotic birds are kept in the park aviary, there are penned areas for goats and chickens, a butterfly dome and a deer enclosure.

Clissold Park
Green Lanes
London, N16 9HJ

❷ Kew Gardens

Kew Gardens
Richmond
Surrey, TW9 3AB

020 8332 5655
www.kew.org

With over 1 kilometre of gardens, the largest collection of plants in the world, seasonal events and a long list of child-friendly attractions, Kew Gardens is the perfect place to introduce children to all manner of botanical life. Kids aged three to nine will enjoy clambering insect-sized around the *Honey I Shrunk The Kids*-style botanic-themed, indoor playground Climbers and Creepers, where they can learn about our relationship to plants.

Outdoors there is the Log Trail and Treehouse Towers—swings, tepee tents, scramble nets, slides and rope bridges comprise this adventure playground surrounding three towers, off of which courageous kids will enjoy zip-wiring. On top of all that—literally—is the Xstrata Treetop Walkway, a path immersed 18 metres high in the trees amongst birds, insects, lichen, blossom and fungi that is difficult to spot down below. Bear in mind that there are 118 steps up to the 200-metre long walkway.

In the southwest corner of Kew Gardens there is another super-sized feature—an enlarged subterranean badger sett in which visitors are welcomed to explore an enlarged food store, sleeping chambers and nests connected by labyrinthine tunnels.

❸ Crystal Palace Park

Crystal Palace Park—the vast green expanse that surrounded the glass Great Exhibition building until it famously burnt down in 1936—comprises a children's play area, miniature farm, former boating lake, fishing lake, sports centre and concert bowl. As well as exceptional views across the city, quirky features of the now palace-less park include the city's largest maze (which, with walls only three feet high, you don't have to worry about losing anybody in) and the loved dinosaur trail—a park path lined with an assortment of somewhat oddly shaped, giant Victorian dinosaur models dating from Prince Albert's original exposition.

Thicket Road
Crystal Palace
London, SE19 2GA

London Wetland Centre
Queen Elizabeth's Walk Barnes
London, SW13 9WT

020 8409 4400
www.wwt.org.uk/wetland-centres/london/

The London Wetland Centre is an important area of conservation for much of the wetlands around the capital. Just ten minutes from Hammersmith, West London, the Centre covers an astonishing area; its lakes, ponds, gardens and wetlands are home to a large assortment of wildlife, including a fascinating collection of international water birds and a family of otters. These animals, along with a variety of species that were previously near extinct, are provided homes in the wetlands, which are vital for such wildlife as well as our own drinking water. The important protection of these areas is carried out by the Wildfowl & Wetlands Trust (WWT) conservation charity, which also researches how to preserve them for the future.

Family visits to London Wetland Centre will get urban kids in touch with nature; in the Discovery Centre they can learn about the wetlands of the world through a number of stimulating games, including both real pond dipping and exploring the Centre's 'digital pond'. In addition there is an adventure playground with zip-wires, climbing wall and appropriately, water games.

⑤ New River Walk Path

From Stoke Newington to Islington

Though the 28-mile long waterway along which this path runs is called the "New River", it is actually historic, having been opened in September 1613.

For kids, following the New River Walk provides an excellent opportunity to observe nature and wildlife around the 400-year-old path; in the many years since its construction, the Heritage section of the path has allowed for wildlife to flourish, and kids can effortlessly point out ducks, coots and many other animals that call the area home. During the winter, the river often freezes, giving the path a different look of beauty in the cold months. The New River Path is an excellent destination for those looking to take their children on a low-stress, leisurely stroll through one of London's most organic and scenic locations.

⑥ Nature Play

Nature Play
Highgate Woods/ Sydenham Woods

www.nature-play.co.uk

Meeting regularly in both Sydenham and Highgate Woods, Nature Play offer play sessions with a difference. These gatherings provide the perfect opportunity to give kids contact with nature in some of the city's wilder spots, with an emphasis on "child-led play" (allowing children to explore, interact and move autonomously without direction), which also offers an excellent learning experience.

Though you are present to support and keep them safe, Nature Play encourage a type of play session in which your child is allowed to explore freely, discover their own abilities or limitations, and develop their own experiences—and therefore, their own knowledge. Simply by standing back, observing and seeing what unfolds, you provide space enough for your child to follow their own urges, and learn how to problem solve independently. Doing so in some of London's natural environments, children will learn about nature and the ecosystem, garner a curiosity and respect for the wilderness, and develop their imagination and creativity. No need to bring toys on these trips, the Woods provide ample natural stimuli!

It is free to join these sessions, but check the website beforehand, as places are limited so as to keep the session safe and calm.

⑦ Victoria Park

Victoria Park
Grove Road
Bow
London, E3 5TB

www.towerhamlets.gov.uk/victoriapark

Opened in 1845, Victoria Park is one of the oldest parks in London, and remains a fantastic location for kids to spend the day. This East End favourite underwent a refurbishment in 2012 that updated many of its elements, including the children's playground, which now has several fun and unique elements, such as rope swings, fountains and a pirate ship. As well as beautiful botanic gardens and a mini golf course, the Park contains a large amount of green space to run around, paths to bike along, and is home to three different lakes. The Model Boat Lake, next to the Splash Playground, houses the oldest Model Boat club in the world, and the Victoria Model Steam Boat Club holds upwards of 17 regattas at the lake every year.

⑧ Gunnersbury Nature Triangle

Gunnersbury Triangle
Bollo Lane
Gunnersbury
Greater London, W4 5LW

www.wildlifetrusts.org/reserves/
gunnersbury-triangle

A triangular plot carved out by three crossing railway lines that cut through West London has, after being left to the elements since the Second World War, become an organic area of inner-city wilderness. Since the early 1980s the spot has been retained as a nature reserve, and is now 'maintained' by London Wildlife Trust Volunteers. Consisting of birch and willow woodland with marshland, a meadow, and numerous ponds too, Gunnersbury Nature Triangle is open to the public daily. Amongst the Triangle's residents are hedgehogs, birds, field voles and insects, and numerous educational signs give further information about the wildlife at various points of interest. Kids will love escaping into the wild at Gunnersbury—only the distant sounds of passing cars or intermittent trains grumbling along the bordering tracks remind you of the city that literally surrounds the reserve—but should be supervised, as tangled nature trails lead in all directions throughout its expanse.

Arts & Entertainment

Film

ACTION

The British Film Institute's South Bank bolthole—the go-to place for contemporary British and World Cinema—isn't just for those involved in the film industry. In fact, bringing the art of cinema to wider audiences is one of the BFI's primary concerns and on their monthly Family FUNdays this applies to adults and children alike. With a family film screening of anything from silent classics by Charlie Chaplin to brand new Hollywood releases, and a follow-up, themed workshop, the FUNdays really are a fun and sociable activity for kids who love film.

The British Film Institute
Belvedere Road
South Bank
London, SE1 8XT

0207 928 3232
www.bfi.org.uk

Rich Mix
35–47 Bethnal Green Road
London, E1 6LA

0207 613 7498
www.richmix.org.uk

Kids' Cine Time (regular Saturday and Sunday morning family film showings) and Parents and Baby screenings every Monday are just two of the features on Rich Mix's programme of child-friendly film events (supported by helpful family discount tickets). Additional activities for children of all ages include extensive imagination-stimulating take-part sessions in arts and crafts, music, performance and movement. Storytelling is also on offer at the cinema with StoryCraft—story time for parents or guardians and children aged between two and five, led each time by a different storyteller or poet.

③ Ritzy

The Ritzy Picturehouse
Brixton Oval
Coldharbour Lane
London, SW2 1JG

0871 902 5739
www.picturehouses.co.uk

The Ritzy Picturehouse, has a host of film-based activities to keep children of all ages entertained. The Kids' Club, held every Saturday morning, is for anybody aged three to 12; kick off the day with fun activities, such as face painting, dressing-up and drawing, before settling in to watch a movie—anything from a recent hit to a classic favourite or family-friendly piece of World Cinema.

At the Ritzy there is also short Toddler Time screenings and the weekly—aptly named—"Big Scream" parents and baby screening.

Children over eight can be left at the Kids Club screenings. However, though additional precautions are taken (such as increased staffing and only entry for over 18s who are accompanying a child), be aware that the cinema is not providing official childcare.

Storytelling

① Tales on Moon Lane

Tales on Moon Lane
25 Half Moon Lane
London, SE24 9JU

020 7274 5759
www.talesonmoonlane.co.uk

As well as a beautiful selection of children's books, the delightful Tales on Moon Lane has a plethora of attractions to engage young children in stories and language. As well as storytelling sessions for pre-schoolers and phonics classes during term time, the bookshop hosts its own festival of events every half term and one-off signings with children's authors throughout the year. Like Tales on Moon Lane, many bookshops and local libraries host various reading and story-themed events, so make sure to look into those near you.

❷ Barbican Children's Library

Barbican Library
Silk Street
London, EC2Y 8DS

020 7628 9447
www.barbican.org.uk

Barbican Children's Library has plenty of books, audiobooks and DVDs to borrow, spaces for kids to read inside and computers with filtered Internet access. The Library also has regular storytelling events including: rhymetime sessions (half an hour of reading for children and parents, with stories, rhymes and music) which run every Monday morning for those between 18 months and three years of age, and every Friday morning for those aged 18 months and under; and storytime—a fun story session which aims to introduce those between three and five years of age to socialising with their peers—every Monday afternoon.

❸ The National Gallery

The National Gallery
Trafalgar Square
London, WC2N 5DN

0207 747 2885
www.nationalgallery.org.uk

The National Gallery has a unique, interactive storytelling event held every Sunday at 10.30 am (repeated again at 11.30 am). For each of the weekly "Magic Carpet Storytelling" sessions an intricate Persian rug 'lands' in front of a different painting for a story. Recommended for children aged between two and five years old, the sessions last half an hour, but could inspire endless adventures discovering your own stories around the Gallery.

④ Discover Children's Story Centre

The Discover Children's Story Centre
383–387 High Street
Stratford
London, E15 4QZ

020 8536 5555
www.discover.org.uk

The Discover Children's Story Centre is a haven for nurturing the imaginations of children aged 11 and under. An indoor "Story Trail" is lined with play cues and props, including a tea party scene, a secret cave, giant's legs, a magical tower slide and dressing-up costumes. At the Discover Children's Story Centre, kids can slide down a monster's tongue, climb on a spacecraft and play with giant musical instruments in the Story Garden.

A programme of immersive exhibitions—each designed by different book illustrators—in the Story Studio allows you to become the main character in a story scene, with past themes including everything from a monster city, superheroes and pirates, to secret agent missions.

There is also an abundance of storytelling and reading events at the Centre; story sessions can take place in the garden's "Story Glade"; Discover Story Builders is an interactive storytelling event based on favourite books; and the Centre's annual literature festival—The Big Write—invites authors and illustrators to talk about their latest stories in a programme of fun and inspiring events.

Of course, all of these exciting opportunities make the Centre not just a destination for getting lost in stories, but also an incredible place to play.

Theatres

❶ artsdepot

artsdepot is a hub of arts activity for children in Finchley, North London. At artsdepot an impressive programme of performances and exhibitions for audiences of all ages is complemented by a catalogue of classes and workshops for everyone from preschoolers to young people in the youth theatre, including "messy play", dance, music and performance.

artsdepot
5 Nether Street
Tally Ho Corner North
Finchley
London, N12 0GA

020 8369 5454
www.artsdepot.co.uk

② Battersea Arts Centre

Battersea Arts Centre has an interesting mix of arts activities that aim to engage the entire community, including an annual agenda of performances and workshops for family fun and creative learning. The Centre gives visitors the chance to experience innovative and engaging forms of theatre; many of Battersea's productions deviate from conventional set-ups by inviting the audience to discover plays in unusual locations, such as throughout the Centre's former town hall building or the local area, for example. Children—who may usually be expected to sit in a dark and quiet auditorium—will enjoy experiencing this very different type of performance.

Battersea Arts Centre
Lavender Hill
London, SW11 5TN

0207 223 2223
www.bac.org.uk

The Battersea Arts Centre has its very own indoor playground too (see p 119).

The Little Angel Theatre
14 Dagmar Passage Off Cross Street
Islington, N1 2DN

0207 226 1787
www.littleangeltheatre.com

The Little Angel Theatre is a tiny treasure trove for the imagination, set behind Islington's Upper Street. Established in 1961, the theatre has been conjuring up magical worlds for children and families for over 50 years. What makes the Little Angel Theatre particularly special is its dedication to the art of puppetry. The theatre hosts various internationally touring live animation productions as well as their own—and the Little Angel Theatre's home-grown productions truly are their own; adjoining the auditorium is a workshop in which all of their puppets are lovingly hand created.

As well as enjoying the shows, children can try their own hands at puppetry in various eight-week long Saturday morning clubs at the theatre. For the very youngest puppeteers, aged between two and five years (and their accompanying guardian), the theatre's Crafty Kids programme is an introduction to simple puppet making, as well as various crafts, songs and games all linked to the theatre's current production. The Saturday Puppet Club for children aged between five and 11 years (split into younger and older groups) sees them undertake a course of creating both their own puppets and production, which they perform for friends and family in the theatre at the end of the course. For children aged 11 and up, the Little Angel Youth Theatre focuses on puppetry performance skills, eventually leading to their very own puppet cabaret evening in which they'll demonstrate how a puppet tells a joke, swallows a sword or even walks a tightrope.

❹ Puppet Theatre Barge

Set on a converted barge, this little marionette playhouse guarantees a unique and memorable theatrical experience. The Puppet Theatre Barge, which is moored at Richmond-Upon-Thames in the summer and Little Venice throughout the rest of the year, specialises in live animation for all ages, with an excellent programme for productions that will appeal to children in a quirky surrounding to suitably ignite the imagination.

The Puppet Theatre Barge
Moored at Little Venice
Blomfield Road (opposite no 35)
London, W9 2PF

0207 249 6876
www.puppetbarge.com

⑤ Polka Theatre

Polka Theatre
240 The Broadway
Wimbledon
London, SW19 1SB

0208 543 4888
www.polkatheatre.com

Polka has specialised in theatre for audiences aged up to 14 years since opening in 1979. Now over 90,000 children visit its two theatres—the Main Theatre and the Adventure Theatre—every year to see funny family shows, child-centered dramas, world premieres and adaptations of well-loved classics. Children as young as nine months old are catered for at Polka, where sensory and visual interpretations of simple stories are put together as imaginative productions that introduce children to theatre.

Polka also has an out-of-school programme of activities for children and families, a garden, playground and book corner, and a particularly impressive scheme of inclusion comprising performances with fully integrated sign language; touch tours of the stage, set and actors; and 'relaxed performances'.

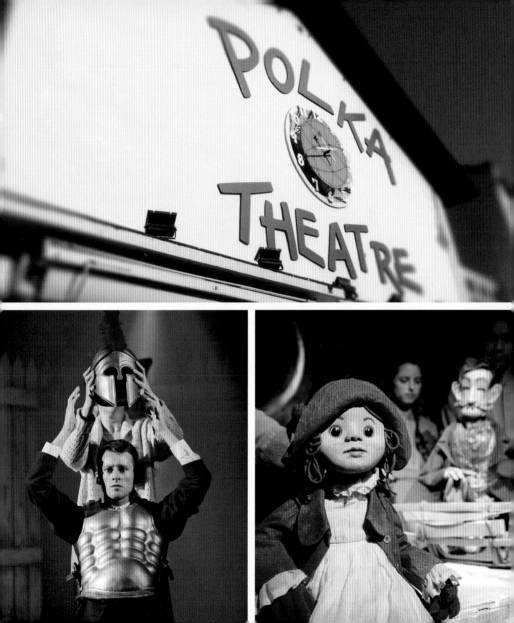

Creating Things

Little Hands Design

Let kids with a budding interest in fashion try their hands at all aspects of fashion design, from planning and making their own clothes or accessories, using patterns, surface design, sketching and illustrating, to upcycling materials, amongst other things, with Little Hands. In these weekly after school and weekend classes (as well as some drop-in sessions and holiday-time crash courses), students will garner a core knowledge of process and basic skills so they can develop their own designs and creations. All tools and fabrics are provided for the sessions, though those taking part are welcome to bring along their own materials to experiment with.

Little Hands Design
67 Belsize Lane
London, NW3 5AU

020 7431 0573
www.littlehandsdesign.com

Get messy and creative at ZEBRA Ceramics, a place that combines pottery painting fun with a quality cafe setting. First, pick an item from a huge range of ceramic items including picture frames, money boxes and vases; children may enjoy creating a character with a ceramic figurine, or decorating their own tea time plates and bowls. Then, using special—washable and non-toxic!—paints, sponge, splash, splodge, dot and draw your own design onto your chosen item. And if your child is particularly ambitious, technicians are on hand to help with creative ideas and techniques. Once you're happy with the final design, ZEBRA will glaze and fire the item, and after ten days you can pick up the glossy final product, ready to use.

When you have finished painting, why not sit back in the cafe with a coffee and one of ZEBRA's tempting cakes while the kids enjoy the indoor or outdoor playing areas.

All ZEBRA ceramics are dishwasher proof and have been tested for food safety. A studio fee of £5 per painter covers all of the processing, firing and material costs, and ceramic items range in price from £3 to £40. It is recommended you book a table in advance on busy periods, such as Saturdays and school holidays.

ZEBRA Ceramics
110 Alexandra Park Road
Muswell Hill
London, N10 2AE

0208 442 1314
www.zebraceramics.co.uk

The Strings Club
Various Locations

07799 33 2562
www.thestringsclub.org

Learning to play an instrument in a group can be a fun and social introduction to music for children. The Strings Club offers such classes in violin, guitar, cello and ukulele. Their "Sound Start" programme introduces children to one of these instruments over a ten-lesson course which culminates in a grand concert—a real goal for the children, who will learn valuable lessons in teamwork, social skills and the basics of music, including rhythm, pitch, notation and dynamics. Very early starters, aged four, can begin with the Strings Club Minis Ukulele, where they will be introduced to the basics of listening, appraising and performing while building confidence, making friends and having a fun, memorable experience.

As well as running throughout the year, The Strings Club hosts school holiday clubs with a full programme of musical workshops from instrument making to composing.

The Kids' Cookery School
107 GunnersburyLane
Acton
London, W3 8HQ

020 8992 8882
www.thekidscookeryschool.co.uk

The Kids' Cookery School introduces young minds to wellbeing—the healthy recipes behind these hands-on classes equip kids with both skills for the kitchen and an early understanding of how to live a balanced lifestyle too. The lessons and more substantial workshops take place in special teaching kitchens in West London, and are open to all children aged between three and 14 years (separated into age appropriate groups), including those with special needs or requirements. With a delicious final product to bring home (and eat!), these little chefs will come away with new talents, knowledge and a real sense of achievement.

Weekly hosts of a Hackney-based arty after school club for kids aged five to 11, ARTBASH also put on a special week-long creativity extravaganza in their annual ARTBASH Camp at altering museums around the capital. During the camp, a number of creative workshops—some outside, if the weather is agreeable!—revolve around a theme that is artfully linked to the host museum's current show. Using a range of recycled materials, ARTBASH encourage kids to get innovative and creative, and as it is run by a group of practicing artists, they will do all of this through a combination of traditional and experimental art making methods. As well as leaving having had a fun-packed week, kids will come home with a number of their own masterpieces to display. Children can attend ARTBASH Camp either in full or for select days. See their website for more details.

ARTBASH
Various Locations

07966132209
www.artbash.co.uk

The Creation Station
Various Locations

0844 854 9100
www.thecreationstation.co.uk

The Creation Station runs arts and crafts classes for children all over the capital. Divided into three age groups, the classes cater for everyone from three months to 11 years, and invite parents along for the adventure too. As well as preparing children for early learning by engaging their curiosity, creativity and imagination, the sessions are an opportunity to have messy fun with your child without the clearing up afterwards!

For earliest stage exploration the Baby Discovery Classes (for ages three to 18 months) open up the senses via new textures, colours and shapes. Little Explorers Classes (for those aged 18 months to five years) move children on to activities, such as playing with slimy clay, printing their own flags and making salt dough "friendship rainbows". Each of the classes, which centre around "the magical ideas box" from which new materials and creative ideas emerge, allow little participants to develop confidence, creativity and turn their hand to experimental problem solving. Lastly, Family Fun classes—which run during the school holidays—are for anybody aged 11 and under. With a similar mix of themes, materials and tools, these are excellent for keeping the kids entertained during holiday time.

⑦ The Big Draw

The Big Draw
Various Locations

www.thebigdraw.org

The Big Draw is an annual celebration of drawing organised by The Campaign for Drawing—a charity that endeavours to give the medium credence as a means of communication and innovation, whose patrons include Quentin Blake and David Hockney.

Over the weeks of the festival everyone has the chance to get drawing—including those who feel hopeless with a pencil—and having recently partnered up with the Family Arts Festival, The Big Draw has more events on offer across the capital than ever before. An extensive programme of family-friendly drawing events across London's museums and outdoor spaces welcome children to learn more about the art and its possible applications. Institutions that have participated previously include the Victoria and Albert Museum, The British Library, the London Canal Museum, the Queen Elizabeth Olympic Park, the Wellcome Collection and the National Portrait Gallery, amongst many others.

Activities & Leisure

Playgrounds

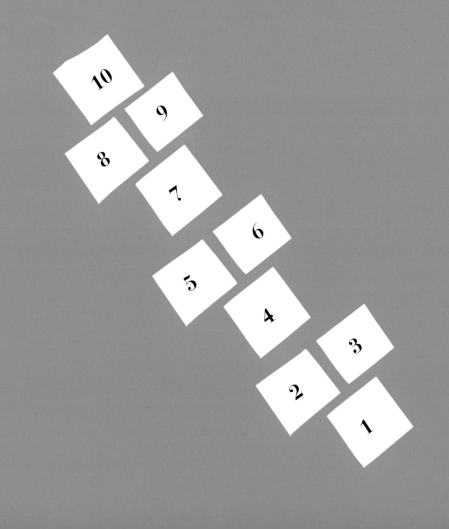

❶ Shakespeare Walk Adventure Playground

Shakespeare Walk
Adventure Playground
Shakespeare Walk
London, N16 8TB

0207 249 8405

On North London's Shakespeare Walk, in leafy Stoke Newington, there is an inclusive, accessible and award-winning playground that has been bringing the children of the area together for over 36 years. Not only does Shakespeare Walk Adventure Playground have both an indoor and an exciting outdoor playground, which render playtime free from weather restrictions, it also has an abundance of extra activities such as a sensory room, soft playroom, fire pit, arts and crafts, gardening, den building and much more.

② The Diana Memorial Playground

The Diana Memorial Playground sits on a corner of Hyde Park next to Kensington Palace, the home of the late princess in whose memory the playground was founded. Based on the adventures of ever-young Peter Pan, the playground is an arena for children to create stories of their own; an enormous wooden pirate ship on a sandy and rocky beach is the main prop on this imaginative set that also includes a ring of tepees, a sensory trail and a sculpture of the story's famous characters.

The free playground is extremely popular and operates a queuing system with a considerable waiting time on sunny days. Make the most of your day by getting comfortable at the Diana Playground Cafe.

It is worth keeping in mind that like The Diana Memorial Playground most playgrounds operate a system whereby any visiting adults must be accompanying a child. Many also require adults to supervise any playing children, though some will allow unsupervised children who register as play members first. Please see the playgrounds' websites for further details.

The Diana Memorial Playground
The Broad Walk
London, W2 2UH

https://www.royalparks.org.uk

❸ Coram's Fields

Coram's Fields
93 Guilford Street
London, WC1N 1DN

www.coramsfields.org

Coram's Fields is one of the capital's favourite playgrounds. Founded over 70 years ago, many grown-ups who loved the park as children still return today, bringing along their own children, or even their grandchildren! Coram's Fields was built on the site of the Foundling Hospital, and several of the Hospital's original Grade II listed Georgian colonnade buildings still surround the play area. Today the playground also features a small city farm area with goats, chickens, rabbits and birds; a community nursery; an out of school club; and a sports programme, amongst other things. Coram's Fields isn't just for little children though, a youth centre and activity programme offers plenty for young teenagers too.

❹ The Bees Knees

Hidden inside the Battersea Arts Centre is an indoor fantasy world for babies and children under five, who will enjoy running up and rolling down the playground's soft green hills. The cute scene—complete with little bridge— is straight from a children's cartoon, and with toys, books and activity tables too, this quirky spot is the perfect play place for budding imaginations. For more information on other offerings from the Battersea Arts Centre, see p 86.

The Bees Knees
Battersea Arts Centre
Lavender Hill
London, SW11 5TN

0207 223 2223
www.bac.org.uk

⑤ The Wild Kingdom

The Wild Kingdom
Three Mills Green
Newham
London, E3 3DU

www.threemillsplayspace.org.uk

Designed by the architectural practice We Made That as a part of the London 2012 Olympic Games' legacy, The Wild Kingdom is a play space that aims to give children exciting adventurous play that isn't divorced from nature. The park, on the renovated landscape of Three Mills Green, is expertly scattered with playground furniture beautifully constructed with combinations of organic and neutral manufactured materials, spaces that embrace the seasons, and play structures such as granite chalk boards, wooden balancing beams, the "Clamberable Canopy" and the "Lookout Log".

Swimming

London Fields Lido

In the northwest corner of London Fields, Hackney, is an Olympic-sized outdoor swimming pool. All 50 metres of the London Fields Lido is open and heated all year round—whatever the weather. Operating with lanes throughout the day, there are plenty of swimming lessons for children available at the lido, and a large sun deck where parents can soak up some sun too. Be warned though, the lido is rightly popular, and sunny days can get extremely busy.

London Fields Lido
London Fields West Side
Hackney
London, E8 3EU

0207 254 9038
http://www.better.org.uk/leisure/london-fields-lido#/

② Hampstead Heath

Hampstead Heath Bathing Ponds
London, NW5 1NA

http://www.cityoflondon.gov.uk/things-to-do/green-spaces/hampstead-heath

Taking to the Hampstead Heath bathing ponds on sunny days in the capital has become somewhat of a summer tradition for Londoners; the three pools—men's, women's and mixed—are outdoor, unheated and untreated swimming pools, which attract hardy, year-round wild swimmers as well as summertime splashers. Though the men's and women's ponds are rather more adult, the mixed pond can be a fun and quirky spot, buzzing with all sorts of people (and pets!).

The ponds are best reserved for bigger kids—only those aged eight or over are allowed, and under 16s will need to be accompanied by an adult—but there are plenty of swimming options for younger children on Hampstead Heath. Parliament Hill Lido, for example, is a large, popular, unheated outdoor swimming pool with excellent views across the city.

For anyone under ten not ready to dive in, the Hampstead Heath paddling pool in the play area is a perfect spot for refreshing aqua play. Open from the beginning of June to the end of August, this summer season walk-in pool is shallow enough for toddlers to stomp and splash about in. Proper swimwear is expected.

If you are heading to Hampstead Heath for the day, it is worth bearing in mind its many other recreational activities for children; as well as swimming, walking paths, playgrounds and gardens are abundant, as are sporting areas, trees to climb and open spaces to run around in.

❸ Diana, Princess of Wales Memorial Fountain

The Princess Diana of Wales Memorial Fountain
Hyde Park
Carriage Drive
London, W2 2UH

https://www.royalparks.org.uk

The Diana, Princess of Wales Memorial Fountain in Hyde Park is a great makeshift splash-about paddling pool for young children. The fountain opened in 2004 to great controversy—it cost a fortune, and the public were not supposed to enter it. Inevitably this request was somewhat ignored, and it is now accepted that people—particularly kids—will clamber in when the weather permits. In fact, as a result the fountain is supervised for safety when open, and closed off during particularly cold or severe weather patches.

The fountain is shaped in a large loop, at the top of which water starts to flow down in both directions until it reaches a still pool at the base. Along the way the water swirls, ripples and bubbles up along sections of granite carved with different shapes and surfaces, making it great for adventurous children to walk around. It is also welcomed by mums and dads, who can cool their feet in the water too. Be sure to keep close to small kids, the wet granite can get slippery.

❹ Oasis Sports Centre

Oasis Sports Centre Outdoor Pool
32 Endell Street
Covent Garden
London, WC2H 9AG

0207 831 1804
http://www.better.org.uk/leisure/
oasis-sports-centre#/

Situated in the middle of Covent Garden, just moments from Shaftesbury Avenue, the outdoor swimming pool at Oasis Sports Centre is likely London's most unexpected. But, as surprising as it is, there have actually been public baths of some sort on this spot since the nineteenth century. Perfect for a fun activity on a day out in the centre of town, Oasis has both outdoor and indoor pools, both of which are open all year round. The outdoor pool can get busy in the summer with local office workers emerging daily for refreshing lunchtime dips, but there is no need to be brave in the calmer, colder months—it's heated. Part of the patio area surrounding the pool is dedicated to families and there is a cafe in the complex serving smoothies and ice creams.

⑤ Leyton Leisure Lagoon

With a water flume for children over eight, an "aqua play area" for those under eight, Tot's Water World drop-in sessions for the under fives, and designated fun and family swim sessions, the Leyton Leisure Lagoon—now part of the Leyton Leisure Centre—is an entire aqua adventure for children and families. The specially designated teaching pool also makes the Leyton Leisure Lagoon a particularly good place for early swimmers, and its swimming classes for children starting as young as three months old are supported by a great inclusion programme, including disability swimming lessons.

Leyton Leisure Lagoon
763 High Road
Leyton, E10 5AB

0208 558 8858
http://www.better.org.uk/leisure/leyton
-leisure-centre/page/264

⑥ London Aquatics Centre

London Aquatics Centre
Olympic Park
London, E20 2ZQ

0208 536 3150
http://londonaquaticscentre.org/

Part of the legacy from London's 2012 Olympic staging, the London Aquatics Centre in the Queen Elizabeth Olympic Park is a place for the public to get involved in sport. The impressive facilities at the centre include three pools; an Olympic size (50 metres) competition pool; a training pool (also 50 metres), which is often divided between lane and fun swimming; and a diving pool with several platforms and springboards. In fact, diving is a particular focus of the centre's, and it also has dry training facilities, including trampoline springboards, foam pits and harnesses. Young fans will be excited to learn that the London Aquatics Centre is the training location for British world class diver Tom Daley, and the Tom Daley Diving Academy—with a programme for Junior Divers aged between five and 16 years—is based here, with classes operating from the same pool that the Olympic medallist trains in twice a day.

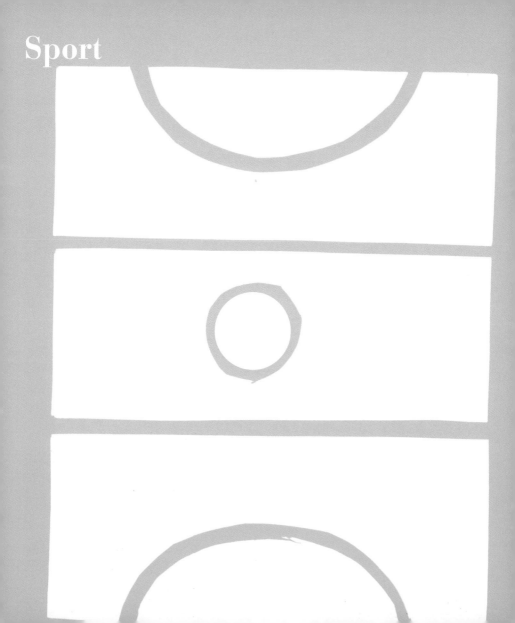

Sport

Children from five years old can learn to ride a horse in the capital at the Hyde Park Stables. They offer lots of options, including technique, dressage or jumping lessons in their arena, but perhaps their most exciting is a ride through Hyde Park itself. These are offered in groups, as individual lessons, or even as parent and child sessions. Hyde Park Stables also host half-day camps in which participants spend an hour riding in the park, an hour learning technique in the arena, and an additional hour learning everything about horse care in the stables. No previous riding experience is necessary to take part in the stables' year-round programme, and they have a family of friendly horses and ponies to fit all sizes.

Hyde Park Stables
63 Bathurst Mews
London, W2 2SB

0207 723 2813
www.hydeparkstables.com

② Brooklyn Bowl

Brooklyn Bowl
The O2
Peninsula Square
London, SE10 0DX

0207 412 8778
www.brooklynbowl.com

Brooklyn Bowl, in The O2, is a bowling alley with a difference. As well as 12 bowling lanes and American-style food, the venue is also home to a performance area where live music acts can provide the backdrop to a game. Children are only allowed into the venue until 7 pm (at the weekends the venue opens at midday), when the bar opens, but with its contemporary décor, huge area for running around, children-sized shoes, bowling aids and familiar children's food menus, it is a cool take on the classic family activity.

③ Roller Disco

From 11 am to 5 pm every Saturday in Vauxhall, people of all ages can get their skates on at the Family Jam—a daytime roller disco. Suitable for novices or the well practiced, the Family Jam is fun and safe, with experienced instructors to help guide those less confident in the rink. There is plenty of seating areas for spectators, or for skaters to refuel, and there are booths that can be booked out for larger parties. At the Family Jam children must be supervised, and all adults must be accompanied by a child.

Roller Disco (Family Jam)
Miles Street
London, SW8 1RZ

www.rollerdisco.com

National Centre for Circus Arts
Coronet Street
London, N1 6HD

0207 613 4141
www.nationalcircus.org.uk

The National Centre for Circus Arts is a hub of exciting physical activities for children as young as four months old. 12-week courses for those aged two years and up (separated into several similar-age groups) introduce participants to all manner of circus arts, from storytelling, balancing and juggling to acrobatics and tightwire work. Kids don't have to commit to long courses though, the Centre also offers Youth Circus Experience Days for those aged eight and up. In these one-off day workshops the children get to try their hand at the trapeze, diabolo and tightwire, amongst other various circus skills.

Family drop-in classes offer parents the opportunity to try out some circus tricks with their infant, as a form of integrated exercise. Separated into "not yet crawling" and "crawlers up to walkers" groups, these promise to be a unique and active way to spend time with your preschoolers.

⑤ Laburnum Boat Club

Laburnum Boat Club
Laburnum Street
London, E2 8BH

0207 729 2915
http://laburnumboatclub.com/

The Laburnum Boat Club is an inclusive community project based in Hackney, East London. Established in the 1980s, the club has been offering a range of water-based activities ever since, and today also offers some sessions specifically for children, young people and families. The Family Club, which runs on Sunday mornings during term time, gives families the opportunity to enjoy narrowboating and canoeing, while the Boat Club's Youth Club—open to anyone between the ages of nine and 19—has a whole catalogue of sports and activities for children to get involved with. From all of their various watersports, including kayaking and canoeing, to alternative options such as ice skating, cycling, climbing and table tennis, amongst many others, youth club members are bound to have a fun, sociable and active adventure.

The Castle Climbing Centre
Green Lanes
London, N4 2HA

020 8211 7000
www.castle-climbing.co.uk

The Castle Climbing Centre—four floors of varied-level climbing action in an obsolete Victorian pumping station built in the style of a Scottish castle—is considered, amongst those in the business, to be one of Europe's leading indoor climbing destinations. And with over 450 roped and lead routes, and an extensive range of bouldering surfaces, the Castle can offer great opportunities for kids and young people.

As well as weekly climbing clubs for children—N4 for ages nine to 14 years, and N4 Minis for those aged five to eight years old—in which an experienced instructor takes a small group through games and climbing to develop their coordination and balance, as well as increasing confidence, trust, motivation and fitness levels, the Castle Climbing Centre hosts one-off Kids' Fun Sessions and combined classes for children and guardians.

⑦ Alexandra Palace

Alexandra Palace
Alexandra Palace Way
London, N22 7AY

0208 365 2121
www.alexandrapalace.com

Though it sits amidst a number of diverse sporting facilities, such as a skate park, pitch & putt and a boating lake, Alexandra Palace is held in the hearts of Londoners largely for its ice skating—an activity not reserved solely for the festive period, as the Palace's permanent rink demonstrates. Located in this original 1873 building, the skating at "Ally Pally" is open to the public everyday throughout the year.

Events on the rink specifically for children include various courses for those aged five to 15, as well as parent and toddler ice sessions. But an equally fun time can be had as spectators; Alexander Palace is the place for sports fans to catch an ice hockey game in London.

Sightseeing

Tours

① London RIB Voyages

Operated on powerboats nipping at high speed along the Thames, London RIB Voyages' adrenaline-fuelled trips are tours like no others in the city.

It might sound a little scary, but the tours are suitable for families, and any ages are welcome (though it is recommended that pregnant mothers stay ashore). Small children are welcome to sit either next to or on the lap of an accompanying adult, and commentary by trained tour guides takes the age of their audience into account when giving you the lowdown on London's riverside attractions. London RIB Voyages offer a number of tours, but Captain Kidd's Canary Wharf Voyage is perhaps best for families, speeding past London sights for approximately 50 minutes.

All-weather gear is provided on wetter days, and life jackets are available for everyone, including babies, toddlers and small children. Storage is available for pushchairs.

London RIB Voyages
The London Eye Millenium Pier
Westminster Bridge Road
South Bank
London, SE1 7PB

0207 928 8933
www.londonribvoyages.com

② Treasure Trails

Treasure Trails
Various Locations

01872 263692
www.treasuretrails.co.uk

A different take on the city tour is provided by Treasure Trails, who have a huge selection of self-guided, clue-led tours that make learning about the city a fun, interactive experience for children and the family. Angled as a quest, Treasure Trails' written guides play on themes such as spy missions preventing alien invasions, treasure hunts for royal bounty, and detective searches to solve eerie murder mysteries

Treasure Trails are available to download or receive in the post from £6.99, and for a little extra money you can personalise your own version—make your family key characters in the story by inserting your own pictures! Unlike organised walking tours—with tour guides and often in large groups—you can take Treasure Trails at your own pace and make pit stops whenever you need along the way.

❸ TFL Buses

TFL Buses
Various Locations

www.tfl.gov.uk

Hundreds of London's famous red double-deckers wind their way around the city everyday, and many offer a sterling view of the capital from their top decks. Several bus routes are particularly favourable for catching the sights; the Number 11 (get on at Liverpool Street and alight at Chelsea) will take you on a tour past the Bank of England, Westminster Cathedral, Westminster Abbey, the Churchill War Rooms, the Houses of Parliament, Trafalgar Square, the Horse Guards Parade, passing nearby the Royal Exchange, the Royal Courts of Justice, Nelson's Column and Big Ben. Other notable routes include the Number 73 and the Number 15, both of which are similarly landmark-laden and, of course, cheap! Be aware that during peak commuter hours TFL's London buses can be extremely busy.

④ London Duck Tours

London Duck Tours operate city tours in amphibious vehicles—those now ubiquitous bright yellow boats on wheels. Exciting for little children who will enjoy transferring from land to water, the tours are also plainly a quirky way to sightsee in the city. The classic tour, for example, takes in views of many of London's major landmarks—the London Eye, The Houses of Parliament, the Horse Guards, Buckingham Palace and the MI5 Building—all in an hour and 15 minutes, just under half of which is spent in the river.

London Duck Tours
55 York Road
London, SE1 7NJ

0207 928 3132
www.londonducktours.co.uk

RV014

⑤ Muggle Tour

The Muggle Tour

07914 151041
www.muggletours.co.uk

Little witches and wizards will enjoy a Harry Potter-themed walk around the capital. The Muggle Tour, between its start at London Bridge and conclusion in Leicester Square, takes you to memorable locations in the franchise films, from the Leaky Cauldron and the Ministry of Magic to Grimmauld Place, amongst others. At the end of the tour you may even see some real magic!

Though not in partnership with the official Harry Potter machine, the fully independent walking tour has won multiple awards and continues to be a favourite for JK Rowling fans young and old. While any ages are welcome (except babies and very young infants), it is advised not to put anyone under the age of seven through the two and a half hour-long walk, though this is up to parents' discretion. It is also worth checking the diary of the Muggle Tour in advance and booking spaces as the tours are usually kept down to small groups.

The Harry Potter obsessed should also take a trip to Platform 9 ¾ at King's Cross Station. Near an official merchandise shop, where you can stock up on special souvenirs and chocolate frogs, is an excellent photo opportunity: have your picture taken as you disappear onto the mysterious platform, ready to board the Hogwarts Express.

❻ Original Tours

Original Tours
17–19 Cockspur Street
Trafalgar Square
London, SW1Y 5BL

0208 877 1722
www.theoriginaltour.com

One operator of open-topped bus tours around the capital, Original Tours, particularly appeals to those hopping on with small children. As part of their Kids Club, Original Tours offer an activity pack, a London 'passport' in which to collect stamps along the way, and an audio guide specifically made for little listeners, which delivers the tour's factual commentary in fun ways, for example using the voice of the ghost of London.

The Kids Club package is available on two of the company's main sightseeing routes. Both 'hop-on, hop-off', they have over 80 stops around the city and include various Thames and walking tours too. Tickets can be purchased online, or at Original Tours' central London Visitor Centre near Trafalgar Square.

Museums

❶ Museum of London Docklands

Set within a 200-year-old sugar, coffee and rum storage warehouse, the Museum of London Docklands tells the story of the capital's port, the historical trades associated with it and the people who have settled in the area since the Roman period. As well as an intriguing assortment of objects and photographs to explore in the museum's exhibition rooms, there are a number of fun attractions for children, including a soft play area, and a water play area for under-eights in the Mudlarks Gallery.

Museum of London Docklands
No.1 Warehouse
West India Quay
London, E14 4AL

0207 001 9844
http://www.museumoflondon.org.uk/docklands/

❷ London Transport Museum

The London Transport Museum
Covent Garden Piazza
London, WC2E 7BB

0207 379 6344
www.ltmuseum.co.uk

London Transport Museum isn't just for budding train spotters or little transport enthusiasts. The surprisingly fascinating museum, which covers, to an astonishing extent, the history of London, its transport and those who have travelled on it, is becoming a new family favourite in the capital. Exhibits at the Museum include original transport posters and artworks, as well as many authentic London Transport vehicles, old and new.

School holiday-time activities and The Family Station (a permanent installation of age-specific materials and activities to make your visit to the Museum creative and interactive) tailor to the Museum's younger visitors.

On two special Open Weekends a year the Museum's depot in Acton also opens to the public, displaying over 370,000 stored items that span 200 years of the city's history.

The Hunterian Museum

The Hunterian Museum
35–43 Lincoln's Inn Fields
London, WC2A 3PE

0207 869 6560
www.rcseng.ac.uk/museums/hunterian

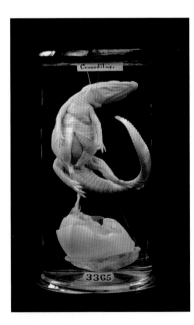

The Hunterian Museum, housed in the Royal College of Surgeons in Holborn, contains the grisly collection of renowned eighteenth century surgeon John Hunter. Hunter took these specimens during his surgical practice as teaching aids. Today, the museum is stacked with all manner of preserved human and animal skeletons, teeth and body parts (including many abnormal or diseased examples).

In addition to the exhibits themselves, there are a number of educational facilities that will appeal to children at the museum: materials for drawing the specimens, anatomical books for children of all ages, and skeleton and organ coats, which display how the wearer's insides fit together. Special holiday events for children include visits from a number of eccentric characters, such as Jones the Bones, a peculiar surgeon who teaches about the human body with the help of his skeleton companion, and Rory McCreadie, a Barber Surgeon, who demonstrates sixteenth and seventeenth century cures, including the use of blood-sucking leeches.

Though all ages are welcome to visit the museum—it is also host to many school groups—it's probably worth bearing in mind that squeamish children might find the displays a little gruesome. Open Tuesday to Saturday, 10 am to 5 pm, the Hunterian is free to visit.

❹ Natural History Museum

Natural History Museum
Cromwell Road
London, SW7 5BD

0207 942 5000
www.nhm.ac.uk

There is an abundance of things to do with kids at the Natural History Museum—an institution which attracts over five millions visitors a year. The striking building houses a number of galleries, including a mammal room (adorned with a life-sized blue whale model suspended from the ceiling), a human biology display and the well-loved dinosaur gallery, amongst many others.

Hands-on sessions, every weekend and during the school holidays from 2–5 pm, allow kids to get up-close to many of the Museum's exhibits, from dinosaur teeth to star fish. These events are ideally for children between the ages of five and 12, but are open to all the family.

The Ragged School Museum
46–50 Copperfield Road
London, E3 4RR

0208 980 6405
www.raggedschoolmuseum.org.uk

During the latter part of the nineteenth century, Dr Barnardo's social awareness movement saw the conversion of several canal warehouses in London's poverty-ridden East End converted into a free school for children of the community. The Ragged School Museum, housed in those buildings, is a faithful reproduction of the original school—the main feature being a true Victorian classroom, complete with authentic desks, slate writing boards, blackboards, easels and dunce hats. Join one of the monthly Sunday lessons with a Victorian teacher dressed in full period attire—just one of many interactive family events at the Museum.

⑥ Tower of London

Tower of London
London, EC3N 4AB

0844 482 7777
http://www.hrp.org.uk/TowerOfLondon/

Arguably one of the capital's favourite visitor destinations, families head to the Tower of London in droves to see the Crown Jewels, the ravens of the Tower and the Beefeaters who guard it. Children's visits could include taking part in some of the family storytelling or activity trails hosted at the Tower, and particularly curious kids may enjoy one of the museum's "archaeology weekends"—a mudlarking treasure hunt on the Tower's Thames beach.

The Charles Dickens Museum

Based in the only remaining London residence of the author and his family, the Charles Dickens Museum at 48 Doughty Street remains exactly as it would have been during the 1830s. Now visitors can experience a little slice of Victorian London in the interactive museum: costumes are available to get them into character, and they can try out many of the period features of the house's kitchen.

As well as a Victorian toy theatre in which they can perform their own productions. There's also an entertaining tour (suitable for children aged six and over) led by the Dickens' housemaid, who may spill a few of the family's secrets along the way; Little Dickens is a popular weekly programme for local families with storytelling, music making and craft sessions (suitable for children under five); and during the school holidays there are fun days with a plethora of authentic activities, such as churning fresh butter to an original Victorian recipe.

The Charles Dickens Museum
48 Doughty Street
London, WC1N 2LX

0207 405 2127
www.dickensmuseum.com

⑧ Horniman Museum and Gardens

Horniman Museum and Gardens
100 London Road
London, SE23 3PQ

0208 699 1872
www.horniman.ac.uk

The Horniman Museum is a wonderful institution which, thanks to its location in Forest Hill, south London, has remained little-known to much of the rest of the capital. Filled with a vast anthropological and zoological collection from the travels of Frederick John Horniman, who generously opened the archive to the public in the nineteenth century, the museum houses a vast array of exotic artefacts, many of which you can touch and explore.

Much of the Museum's permanent collection is still on show, including its famously rotund walrus rather overstuffed by a Victorian taxidermist with no knowledge of such creatures. There are also changing exhibitions, music events and workshops, a well-regarded aquarium and 16 acres of pleasant gardens.

When planning your day out, don't forget the many major, national museums scattered across the capital. Institutions such as the Victoria and Albert Museum, Tate Britain and the Science Museum aren't exactly off the beaten track—in fact, they can conjure quite a crowd—but they offer limitless exciting and educational exhibitions and activities for families, often for free.

One new—and very special—feature on many organisations' interactive event agendas gives kids the opportunity to see many museums after dark; you can now sleep over at the British Museum, the Science Museum and London Zoo, among others. One of our favourites is the Natural History Museum's "Dino Snores" monthly sleepover event for children aged seven to 11. Once its doors have closed, a torch-lit tour of the museum precedes a show about its various inhabitants before a night's sleep under the central hall's resident skeletal Diplodocus. An extraordinary way to experience London's spectacular museums, sleepovers are a unique treat with a rather hefty price tag. Remember to book in advance.

For young sports fans, why not plan a visit to one of the city's sports grounds, many of which offer tours or have on-site museums. Our favourites include the Arsenal Football Museum and Stadium tour, Wimbledon, Marylebone Cricket Club Museum and Lord's Cricket Ground.

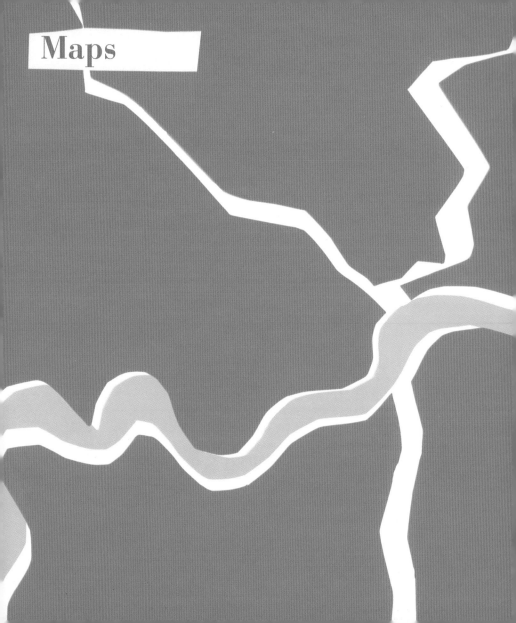

Maps

Central

- London St Pancras International
- Euston Square
- Regent's Park
- Russell Square
- Goodge Street
- Holborn
- Chancery Lane
- Tottenham Court Road
- Piccadilly Circus
- Charing Cross
- Green Park
- Elephant & Castle
- Pimlico
- Kennington

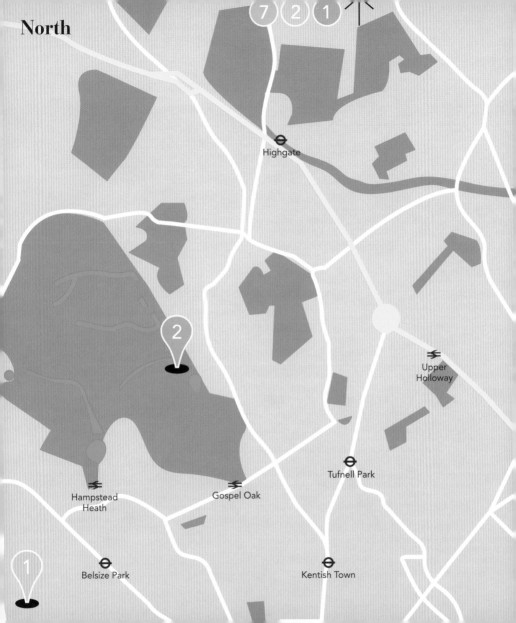

North

Highgate

Upper
Holloway

Tufnell Park

Hampstead
Heath

Gospel Oak

Belsize Park

Kentish Town

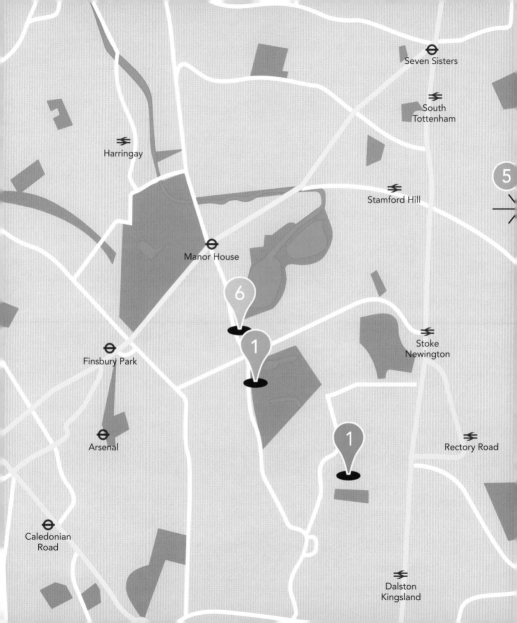

East

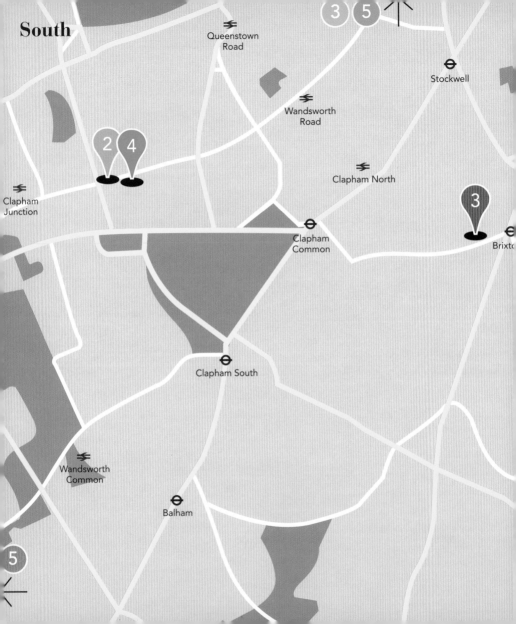

South

Queenstown Road

Wandsworth Road

Stockwell

Clapham North

Clapham Junction

Clapham Common

Brixto

Clapham South

Wandsworth Common

Balham

Loughborough
Junction

North Dulwich

Herne
Hill

1

32

26

30

31

29

27

28

8

Tulse Hill

West Dulwich

3

West

East Acton

Latimer Road

Wood Lane

Holland Park

Shepherd's
Bush

Hammersmith

Barons Court

Image Credits

Cover, clockwise from top left: courtesy Karen Roe, Richard Lea-Hair-HRP-newsteam, Ian Muttoo

p 4: courtesy Donald Judge (cropped)

p 8: courtesy robertsharp

p 9: courtesy Sergio Uceda

p 10 top: courtesy Pittaya

p 10 bottom left: courtesy Kalexander2010

p 10 bottom right: courtesy Daniel Lobo

p 11 top, 13, 20, 21 bottom: courtesy Garry Knight

p 11 bottom: courtesy Chris Marchant

p 14: courtesy Karen Bryan

p 15 top: courtesy Lorenzo G

p 15 bottom: courtesy Michiel Jelijs

p 17: courtesy Byron and Tamara

p 18 top: courtesy Iain Farrell

p 18 bottom left: courtesy Lars Plougmann

p 18 bottom right: courtesy Matt Buck

p 19 top: courtesy The Ministry Of Stories

p 19 bottom: courtesy chrisdb1

p 21 top: courtesy Cristiano Betta

p 22 top: courtesy Rev Stan

p 22 middle, 23, 131 bottom: courtesy Andrea Vail

p 22 bottom: courtesy charity shopper

p 24: courtesy Herry Lawford

p 25 top, 137 top left and bottom right: copyright Ludovic Des Cognets

p 25 bottom: courtesy A Roberts

p 26 top left, 177 top and bottom left: courtesy Horniman Museum and Gardens

p 26 top right, 50 top and bottom: courtesy Ben Sutherland

p 26 bottom, 142: courtesy Matthew Black

p 27, 125 top left: courtesy Tom Page

p 33 left: courtesy S Pakhrin
p 33 right: courtesy MissSaraKelly

p 35–37: courtesy London Aquarium

p 38–39: courtesy Battersea Park Children's Zoo

p 40–41: copyright ZSL London Zoo

p 43–45: courtesy Vauxhall City Farm

p 47: courtesy David Holt London

p 49: courtesy RGB Kew

p 51: courtesy under_volcano

pp 52–53: courtesy Jim Linwood

p 54: courtesy Steve Walker

p 55 top and bottom left: copyright Stephen Morris

p 55 bottom right: courtesy WWT

p 56 left: photograph by Amy Cooper-Wright

p 56 right, 57: courtesy Rachel Pfleger and Dan Neal

p 59: courtesy Clare Caro and Nature Play

p 61 top and bottom left: courtesy eGuide Travel

p 61 bottom right, 62–63: courtesy Vladimir Rogers

p 65: courtesy Bruno Girin

p 69: courtesy BFI_Neil Bird nechbi

p 70–71: courtesy Rich Mix

p 72–73: courtesy Ritzy Cinema

p 75: courtesy Tales on Moon Lane

p 76–77 top and bottom : courtesy Barbican Library

p 78 left and right: © The National Gallery, London

p 79: courtesy Ian Muttoo

p 81 top left and top right: copyright Discover Jeff Moore

p 81 bottom: copyright Discover Andrew Baker

pp 82–83: copyright Discover Tim Mitchel

p 85: courtesy artsdepot

p 86: copyright James Allan

p 87–89, 119: courtesy Battersea Arts Centre

p 90: courtesy Little Angel Theatre

p 91 left and top right: courtesy Antonio Escalante

p 91 bottom right: courtesy Jorge Royán

p 92 left, 93 bottom left: ©Robert Workman

p 92 right, 93 top and bottom right, 94–95: courtesy Polka Theatre

p 97 left and right: courtesy Little Hands Design

p 98 top: courtesy Yvonne Chacraborty

p 98 bottom: courtesy Nemi Miller

p 100–101: courtesy the Strings Club

p 102: courtesy The Kids Cookery School

p 103–105: courtesy ARTBASH

p 107 top left: courtesy The Creation Station and Lou Platt

p 107 top right and bottom: courtesy The Creation Station and Matt Austin

p 109: courtesy The Big Draw

p 113: photography by Shona Noel

p 114 top left, bottom left, bottom right, 115: courtesy Diana Memorial Playground

p 114 top right, 116–117: © Anne Marie Briscombe

p 118: courtesy sara~

p 120, p121 top right: © We Made That

p 121 top left and bottom: courtesy Dan Childs Films

p 123: courtesy Peter Smith

p 123 top right: courtesy insideology

p 123 bottom: courtesy nicksarebi

p 125 top right: courtesy Insideology

p 125 bottom: nicksarebi

p 127 left: courtesy CGP Grey

p 127 top right: courtesy Laura Bittner

p 127 bottom right: courtesy Morgaine

p 130: Courtesy Daniel

p 133: courtesy Hyde Park Stables

p 134: courtesy Brooklyn Bowl (Purple PR)

p 135: courtesy Roller Disco

p 136, 137 top right and bottom left: courtesy Bertil Nilsson

p 139–141: courtesy of Laburnum Boat Club

p 143: courtesy The Castle Climbing Centre

p 144–145: courtesy Alexandra Palace

p 149: courtesy London RIB Tours

p 151: courtesy of Treasure Trails

p 152 left: Dimitry B

p 152 right: ホワイト (shirokazan)

p 153–155: copyright London Duck Tours

p 156: courtesy Steph Magic

p 157: courtesy Karen Roe

p 158–159: courtesy Original Tours

p 161: © Museum of London

p 163: © TfL, from London Transport Museum

p 164–165: ©Hunterian Museum, London

p 166 left: Copyright Natural History Museum

p 166 right: courtesy Allan_ Henderson

p 167: courtesy Mikel Ortega

p 168–171: ©Ragged School Museum Trust

p 172 left, 173 top right: courtesy Richard Lea-Hair/HRP/newsteam

p 172 right: courtesy xiquinhosilva

p 173 top left: courtesy newsteam. co.uk

p 173 bottom: courtesy Tower of London

p 174: ©Charles Dickens Museum

p 177: bottom right: copyright Laura Mtungwazi

p 178–179: courtesy The Trustees of the NHM, London

Acknowledgements

Kids London would not have come to exist in the form it does if it were not for the following: the generous co-operation and imagery contributions from each attraction featured in the book; invaluable editorial support from Phoebe Adler, Thomas Howells, Emine Mahmout, Garrett Schaffel and Kitty Walker; and a clever, playful identity, designed by Freddy Williams. A huge thank you to you all.

Black Dog Publishing Limited
10A Acton Street
London
WC1X 9NG

t.   +44 (0)207 713 5097
f.   +44 (0)207 713 8682
e.   info@blackdogonline.com
w.   www.blackdogonline.com

Edited by Kate Trant and Leanne Hayman, and designed by Freddy Williams
at Black Dog Publishing.

ISBN   978 1 908966 1 31

Black Dog Publishing is an environmentally responsible company.
Kids London is printed on sustainably sourced paper.

art design fashion
history photography
theory and things

black dog publishing

www.blackdogonline.com   **london uk**